Beloved

By the same author:

Nigh
Things I've thought to tell you since I saw you last
Suburban Anatomy
The Unlikely Orchard

Beloved

PENELOPE
LAYLAND

RECENT
WORK
PRESS

Beloved
Recent Work Press
Canberra, Australia

Copyright © Penelope Layland, 2022

ISBN: 9780645356311 (paperback)

Cover image: detail from 'Dora' by Margaret Gillies 1839, reproduced
under licence from The Wordsworth Trust, Dove Cottage, Grasmere
Cover design: Recent Work Press
Set by Recent Work Press

recentworkpress.com

ss

'The dear companion of my lonely walk
My hope, my joy, my sister and my friend,
Or something dearer still, if reason knows
A dearer thought, or in the heart of love
There be a dearer name.'

William Wordsworth (c 1800)

Contents

Contents

Preface

In 1778, when Dorothy Wordsworth was six, her mother died, and young Dorothy was sent to live with a maternal cousin. She never returned to the family home thereafter, even for a visit. Birthdays and Christmases (in Dorothy's case, the same, since she was born on 25 December) were spent apart from her four brothers and father. It was not until their adolescent years, in 1787, that Dorothy and her brothers became reacquainted in any meaningful way. By then, their father too was dead.

As teenagers and young adults, Dorothy and her brother William developed an intense and passionate emotional bond that endured for the rest of their lives. While some further years elapsed before they could put into place their dreams of making a lasting home together, by 1794 they were living together at Windy Brow, in the Lake District of England. From that time, they would rarely be physically separated for more than a few weeks or months at a time, for the rest of their lives.

While their relationship changed over the course of their lives—most significantly after William's marriage in 1802—their attachment remained profound. In 1829, when Dorothy experienced one of the earliest of the bouts of poor physical (and later mental) health that were to blight her later decades, William wrote, 'were she to depart, the phases of my Moon would be robbed of light to a degree that I have not the courage to think of'.

In his poetry William more than once explicitly references his love for Dorothy, and the central role she occupies in his life. On at least one occasion he refashions an incident from their shared life and repurposes it in a poem dealing with a courtship. Some scholars believe that William's strange and beautiful sequence of 'Lucy' poems were also about, or at least inspired by, Dorothy.

The poems in the pages that follow are in the voice of Dorothy. They explore her relationship with her brother at critical points during their shared life—making a home together, their years of close friendship with the poet Samuel Taylor Coleridge, trips to Germany and Scotland, William's marriage to their mutual friend Mary Hutchinson (an event which deeply affected Dorothy) and the decades that followed, with their joys and miseries.

The poems draw for inspiration—and in some cases for individual words or phrases—upon Dorothy's diaries and letters as well as the recollections of friends and family members.

Christmas Day, 1771
Dorothy Wordsworth is born in Cockermouth, Cumberland. Her brother William had been born the previous year, in April.

1778
When Dorothy is six, her mother dies and she is sent to live in Halifax, with her mother's cousin. Her brothers—Richard, William, John and Christopher—remain under the care of their father. Dorothy never returns to her father's house, even for a visit.

December 1783
John Wordsworth, the father of William and Dorothy, dies.

1787
At 15, Dorothy goes to live with
her grandparents in Penrith.

1788
Dorothy goes to live with her
mother's brother,
William Cookson, at
Forncett Rectory, Norfolk.

Spring 1794 Dorothy and her
brother William spend several
weeks at Windy Brow, Keswick,
a property belonging to a friend
of William's. This is the first time
the two have lived under the
same roof since early childhood.

Pledge
(1793)

My hands cannot settle to busy work.
I am hot, though the panes are icy laced
and my eyes go again to the windy door—
each rattle a summons, each summons a battle
for calm.

My brother has sworn he will make us a home—
I own it's what I've always dreamed
and more than I have ever known.
Him too I barely know, in truth,
except in the truth of dreams,
where I live, it seems,
the wind rattling my name.

What makes it—a *home?*
Scarlet beans starting in rows,
food for a starving eye?
The last of winter's shrivelled apples
sweetening another year?
The tones of a voice, unseen but near,
that—even whispered—pierce the ear?

He's a man I've barely seen or known,
yet somehow knows my throbbing heart
in all its sorest, hidden parts.
He vows we shall have a home, together alone,
all in each other.
I kept no home in my heart for hope,
for love, for hearth, for heat, till now.

Letter to Jane Pollard

(July 1793)

Be upon your guard, my friend—
    Read none of this aloud!

You will forgive my writing so much of him—
affection hurries me to a subject for which
you cannot be so hungry as *I*.

Perhaps you will reply
that I am blinded
    —and so I must be,

for *could* a man be all
that my love makes my brother,
or boast one half the brilliance I allow?

Jane—he plans a visit—
    as if by happenstance!

But all may be turned to nought
should any discover our plot.
Say nothing then
    —and excuse this scrawl.
What I have written is mostly blots.

The glance

Entering a room, knowing without looking—
there, in the corner, a withdrawn glance.

Found, foundering, lips move but words
are unheard over the heart's own sound.

He's smiling at someone. Nodding at something.
Now looks. As if by chance.

Letter to Aunt Crackanthorpe from Windy Brow, Keswick

(1794)

I am obliged, Aunt, for your frankness
and sorry—extremely—that you should feel
my conduct such as must be condemned.
Upon what can your sentiments be based,
other than pure baselessness,
and upon—I wonder—*whose* communications?

Can you think me unprotected, when I winter here,
sheltered as a violet under snow
by such a one as my brother?
There could not be another better suited.

And has it become a stain on virtue
to 'ramble on foot', as you put it?
Is not thrift a reason,
or *pleasure*, or use of the native strength
with which God has endowed me?

In mentioning the many inducements I have
to stay a little longer here—
beauty of the country, *pleasantness* of the season—
I will add the society of several of my brother's friends,
from whom I have received the *most friendly* of attentions.

1795
William is introduced to Samuel
Taylor Coleridge in Bristol.

September 1795
Dorothy and William set up
house together at Racedown, in
Dorset, another property owned
by friends of William's. It is here
that Dorothy meets Coleridge
and a strong bond forms between
the siblings and their friend.

July 1797
Dorothy and William move to
Alfoxden, to be closer to their
friend Coleridge. While at
Alfoxden, Dorothy writes what
is now known as the Alfoxden
Journal (written between
20 January and 22 May 1798.

1798
After their lease for Alfoxden is
not renewed, (their unorthodox
behaviour leads some locals to
suspect they are French spies,
and the Admiralty sends an agent
to investigate the possibility)
Dorothy, William and Coleridge
travel to Germany, intending
to learn German and make
money from translation. The
Wordsworths lodge in Goslar.

May 1799
Returning from Germany
Dorothy stays with her friends
the Hutchinsons, at Sockburn.

Coleridge appears at Racedown
(1796)

A being has bounded into our quiet life—
vaulting our low fence,
fording the small torrent of our beck
and breaching all of our defences!

We have let an intruder in,
with his great gift of delighting.

At first, and for minutes only,
I thought him plain—
thick-lipped, hair longish
and of a rough and half-curling black.

But hear him speak and one thinks
no more of skin-deep things,
for his speaking is a river, all depths
and darkness and flashing turns
and when we are together—
William, Coleridge and I—
this river runs quick, dark,
sweet and lovely.

Alfoxden

(1798)

We have been this whole year in a trance,
tracking the Quantock Coombes—
marking each flattened sheep trace,
each cattle meander,
with our haphazard, hob-nail progress.

Coleridge *will* lead, but always strays
or stops too soon—head too full—
to stretch in shade, or beside water. So we pause,
observe, compose, recite, remark, delight,
then on—unwearied, ever.

Seasons have shifted about our heads.
From the tops of the wintering Coombes,
dressed now for the snow
in their flattened grasses,
the west road glitters like a river below.

We hear the sea distinctly now,
which we never could in the hum of summer,
with its breeze among leaves, its busyness of insects,
the redbreast's slender, penetrating notes.

Now, there is only the chill, constant sweep
of water over shingle and the half-deadened sound
of a sheep's bell knocking somewhere
against unseen fleece.

Goslar, Germany, Winter

The year and century wane in deep snow
and black ice. I feel as far from the idea of home
as ever I was—though not, thank God, alone.

To think we dreamed of industry here—
of taking the gems of German prose,
translating them into silver.

But the locals, this hard season, will not converse,
that we may learn how their language is wrought—
or perhaps it is that we, so sufficient,

reluctant to open our door to another,
like creatures numbed,
do not seek the hard lessons taught.

So we stumble through *ja* and *bitte, nein,*
come no closer to fluency than an
infant that can only cry its wants.

Money is short, the cold penetrates every entry.
Coleridge is gone to dazzle Ratzeberg,
where countesses skate on the skin of the lake.

William composes feverishly, but from old memories,
not the now and here. Coleridge writes that, officially,
it is the coldest winter of the century.

December 1799
Dorothy and William set up
house together in Grasmere,
Cumbria. It is here that Dorothy
begins the journal now known
as the *Grasmere Journal* (written
between 14 May 1800 and
11 January 1803).

October 4 1802
William marries Mary
Hutchinson.

The robin poem

A robin chased a scarlet butterfly–
quick red-breast and quicker flitting
against a mild grey sky.

In the orchard, in rising vapours,
I told William what was in my eye
and he wrote the poem
of the robin and the butterfly.

In mist and small rain I took
tea and smaller talk,
leaving him to his walking.
He met me coming back
and read me the changes
he had made to my thought.

Later, out of spirits,
I went to the orchard alone,
saw his half-bitten apples
dropped in the grass.

Unseasonal

Seasons are become unseasonal
and things meant for later life's decay
are brought forward in a rush.

I have lost another tooth.
Soon, all will be gone. This will be past,
yet I will be beloved.

I have never laughed so much!
At the quaintness, the loss of my looks.

Swallows have fashioned their nest on my ledge.
Their white breasts press to my pane
with no awareness of their exposure.

I, in my narrow cot, press belly-down
while my teeth ache and creak
and work free from their home.

The berry

Half-wishing it were so, I happened to say
that as a child I would never pluck a strawberry flower,
for thinking of the berry waiting whitely at its heart.
Now William has ripened my idle talk,
taken my boast, but written me
(as punishment or reward)
a rosier childhood than that I remember—
pinched off, as I was, unfitted,
my white heart shrivelling like a posy.

Trench

Wearied by walking,
we lay in a trench
by a stone fence
and a Laurel tree.
Eyes shut, each unseen
by the other.
He said he could hear
my breathing
and a rustling.
I raised my hands
to block the sun
and through red lids
and red mists fancied
my arms as branches,
fingers as fainter twigs.
Would that I could
have twisted them off
like gloves
and knotted them
into a crown
for my beloved.
When the sun went,
it took such fancies with it.
I grew chilled,
felt each knuckle of my spine
splicing to the soil
with quick roots.
Dreamily, he said
it would be sweet to lie so,

fixed in the grave,
with the sound of water
and birds,
knowing that
dear ones were near.

By firelight

Flames quaver with soft rumbles
and in between, his watch ticks.
No other sound disturbs the hours
of soft dark and wavering shapes
save his breathing, uneven, heaving
at odd times, and then sighing,
as if in relief, as he now and then
pushes forward his book, turns a leaf.

I have walked miles

(Grasmere)

I have walked miles. It is late.
The sky threatens rain, no rain comes, and
no letters wait.

Clouds split, tipping moonlight upon the lake.
I am cold and hungry, mostly.
I have walked miles and it is late.

Only exhaustion can moderate
my hopes. I walk until exhausted.
No letters wait.

I know he has little time, lately
to spare little me. But
I have walked miles and it is late.

I picture him with Mary, heads close. Their lips navigate
sentiments to which I must be deaf.
No letters wait.

It is the cold and the hunger I hate
most. A good, gallant moon helps me home, for
I have walked miles. It is late,
and no letters wait.

The return

I have been a whole day persuaded
he will not come back, will be delayed.

Last night I slept in his bed, but badly—
both dreaming and waking left me afraid.

I have ironed all his collars, and mine,
made pies and sat where we always sit,

walked round the lake in a clashy wind,
come home, tired, to fires unlit.

He came, unexpected, in time for tea.
His mouth and breath were cold when he kissed me.

Coleridge in difficulty

William cannot abide what he calls my *nervous blubbering*
so I sit alone this night, small rubble of fire failing, and
Coleridge's letter impressive as a hot coal in my hand.

What might fate have held for our closed circle
could our friend's steps have been retaken—
and the worst of them forsaken—had his anodyne

not been first taken, and then *taken to*, had he mastered
that welter of emotion, so deeply felt that
it will test even the finest intentions?

Had he met *us*, earlier—discovered another heart
closer vibrating to his wild one than the poor, plain pulse
of the wife I truly pity, feeling even now,

with his words hot in my hand, some small portion
of her indignity. It is for the two,
for their contempt, that I weep.

The swallows' nest

They swim the air, forked fish-tails flashing,
the pair of them hesitating at one eave, then another,
at last choosing mine for their nest.
Ten days I have seen their diligence repaid
in growing ramparts where, of an evening
when it is almost dark,
they will crouch together, twittering low, tremulous.

Last evening was mild and wet
but this morning the nest has fallen
in soft ruins upon my window ledge.
Poor creatures, they dart in alarm and disbelief.
They could not be more distressed.

Today continues rain and very dark.
All the roses are fretted and spoiled.
The peas are beaten down from their trellis.
I have been made sleepless and sick by letters.

Alone at Grasmere

William and brother John
are gone to friends—
to be away *however long*.

I saw them as far as the lake
then farewelled William with a kiss,
then walked, head throbbing,
then sat upon a stone too long—

a series of such slight *thens* as left
the weltering upon the shore
sounding too much like sobbing.

I would have made a visit too,
but am bid to keep a place
to which our friends will gravitate.

By the grate our love sleeps warm
because I keep the fire lit.

Grasmere, twilit, is solemn—
never more so than now.
It calls home my heart
—riotous an hour ago—
to quietness.

The day of his wedding

(October 4, 1802, Gallow Hill)

I kept myself quietly upstairs all the morning
until the knock at the door told it was done,

then found I could stand no more, was flung,
laid out in stillness, unhearing or seeing
until roused by their coming,
a bustle of voices beyond the door.
Then I moved (I know not how
nor how straight) to his breast
and rested there one instant.

Mary was distressed, at the last,
to part from her family.
But after the wedding breakfast
we three departed.
We had brittle sunshine and showers
and some talk and felicity.

I will look well. I will be busy.

Erasure

I gave him the wedding ring—with how deep a blessing!
I took it from my forefinger where I had worn it the whole
of the night before—he slipped it again onto my finger
and blessed me fervently.

The ink bleeds, instantly flooding
words that, once written,
I see must never again be seen, by me
or by him, or any third, but be hidden
as though unwritten. I fetch fresh ink,
do it darkly and well, pressing
the nib deep into my silence—
a fervent assent
to the happiness I must desire.
What could be a higher intent
than to be a third beside that fire?

Home to Grasmere

Rain at the change of horses,
but we made good time
and came to Grasmere just on dark.
I hardly knew my feelings
and was glad, by candlelight,
to roam the garden alone,
marvelling at what change
three months will make,
and that seasons—however cherished—
will delay for no-one.
In the morning we unpacked boxes,
on the Friday baked bread,
then Mary and I walked
the hillside, then the grove end to end,
then hunted waterfalls—
our first walk as sisters
not as friends.

Last entry, Grasmere Diary

(January 1803)

I lay in a drench of sleep till one, then
worked all day on petticoats, wrists,
William's woollen stockings.
We meant to walk
but the furious cold slowed us so,
we ended not walking at all.
Mary read Chaucer's *Prologue* aloud
and since tea has been copying poems.
William works beside me.
I will take tapioca for my supper,
Mary an egg,
William cold mutton.
This book is filled. I will take a new,
and write more regularly.

Here ends an imperfect summary.

June 1803
William and Mary's first child, John, is born. Their other children are Dora (born August 1804) Thomas (born June 1806), Catherine (born September 1808) and William (born May 1810).

August 1803
Dorothy and William leave Mary (and the two-month-old John) and travel to Scotland with Coleridge.

February 1805
The Earl of Abergavenny, a ship captained by Dorothy and William's brother, John, sinks. John is drowned.

June 1812
William and Mary's daughter
Catherine, aged almost four, dies
after suffering convulsions.

December 1812
Six months after Catherine's
death, William and Mary's six-
year-old son, Thomas, dies of
complications from measles.

At the grave of Robert Burns

(Dumfries, Scotland, August 18, 1803)

Seven years dead, and yet no stone,
so we stand, dismayed, at a patch overgrown
by sod, and thick with thistle sown.
       A bed secured
from snow and sun but so alone—
          the man obscured.

The yard is rich with monuments,
fantastic shapes to recompense
in hopeful last emolument.
       One paragraph
—how named, how loved, how lived and whence—
          of epitaph.

The man who'd shown us to the spot
pointed now to a different plot,
a lavish stone with deaths-head topped.
       'A clever man—
Attorney—hardly ever lost!
          A family man.

Your poet made a fine lampoon
upon him once or twice, impugned
him in the way of cheap cartoon.
       But there they rest
as you can see!' He hummed a tune.
          And who's done best?'

No quick recovery from this.
No thought that does not heart-depress.
No cheer that can be wrung—unless
     —despite this grave—
his *song* survive: its sweet caress
       'wild as the wave'.

Sinking of the Earl of Abergavenny
(February 1805)

I summon my hand to write what's said
but my heart will not avow—
off Portland's rocky Shambles
our brother John is dead.

Driven upon rock by a fouling tide,
his ship floated free at the turn,
righted—shifted—sailed—seemed saved—
was filling all the while.

Some dozens who clung to the mizzen mast
are our authority.
John was not with the clinging men—
stood captain to the last.

William will not be consoled for this blow—
creeps, starting at sounds,
pressing his hands to his paining sides,
keeping his eyes turned low,

while I can turn to no shape or shade
that does not summon John—
the orchard trees—placed thus by him,
the hut of moss he made.

But the hut is dank and slimy tonight,
the orchard prisoned in sleep.
No warmth of John's strong hand or breath
survives this frigid fright.

How fearful, tonight, the creek in spate
which startles me awake
to breathless thoughts of seas, and depth,
and paralysing weight.

William flinches from my stroke.
My chimney roars like pain.
Wind and rain drive down the vale.
Our perfect set is broke.

Also lost to that lightless cold:
chests of silver dollars,
bound for Bengal and the alchemy
that would sail them back as gold.

John spun golden tales of wonder,
of freedom from money troubles.
What I would give, this gusty night,
to be tested forever by hunger.

Mean

(1810)

After tea we walked—
my brother ahead
with our visitor
on a narrow track that
barely permitted the two.

Our new friend was massy,
tall too, a telamon
wrenched free
from some pedestal
to walk our simpler earth.

I watched the tableau they made—
one side, my brother's thin
and coltish shanks,
narrow cage,
inky hands and
fine, sparse hair,
a little too long, and lank.

Without his shining face
to lend his usual grace
he seemed to—jerk along.

Was it possible
this was William?
How very mean he seemed.

I cast my eyes about for
some other view,
but in the gloaming
must needs look forward
or down at my legs,
and I was not sorry
when we gained our point
and parted at last
for our separate beds.

Grasmere Churchyard

(December 1812)

So is the soil made perpetually ours,
with the burying of flowers
which too briefly bloomed.

Twice we have come in this year of grief,
offered the ground our grudging gifts.

First, sweet Catherine, in June,
who jumped and skipped
through all her four years and one final
Wednesday afternoon,
yet breathed her last the very next.

She was a most rememberable child.
There are those who put on such shifting shapes
they cannot be called to mind when absent.
She is the same, now, in remembrance
as when she stood, stark alive.

Six months later, a second shock:
Thomas, six, by measles.
Though flushed, feverish, all was favourable,
till eleven on the morning
when the last change came.

His suffering was short, and seemed not so severe.
The result, though, was the same
as if he had struggled far harder.

But he was not one for assertion—
becoming manly, and still yet sweet,
happy to go where—and when—bidden.

We are all in wondering affliction here.
There is no comfort but in the firmest belief
that what God wills for us is best,
though I be too blundering blind to see
in what way that could ever be.

William and Mary are resolved on a removal—
cannot bear the churchyard, glimpsed
a dozen times in an ordinary day.

Where we will go, I cannot say.
I could not so easily think to move,
if it was up to me.

May 1813
The Wordsworth household relocates to Rydal Mount, at Ambleside.

1829
Dorothy experiences her first prolonged bout of ill-health. Despite rallying and enjoying long periods of relatively good health, her physical and mental health decline over the ensuing decades and she spends long periods as a housebound invalid

23 April 1850
William dies.

25 January 1855
Dorothy dies.

Rock of Names

I paused today where once we left our names,
and reckoned how the years might view our mark:
as folly—blunting (for no good) good blades—
or as that spark that man *must* strike from dark?

The years have softened what was then hard-etched
and moss is soft on what's not yet erased
by water such as dipping swallows fetch
from each crevice, uncaring how defaced

the rock at which they flit and bathe and sup.
Dear brother, Mary, me and Coleridge,
our poor dead John and—lowest, though first-cut—
initials scratched to mark a love abridged.

To visit here was long our ritual.
I thought such bonds would prove perpetual.

Final extraction

(1820)

Farewell—out!—the last of my teeth.
Eight there were, including stubs.
The drawing was long, but better than feared
though bad enough.

I've a look of true age in the glass now:
all chin and nose—nothing between.
If my mouth settles in a week
I'm to be measured for a better set.

For fifty sovereigns, a rack of porcelain
brackets, built to fit and last,
steel springs, for speech's simulacrum,
and the ivory—I cannot ask—

whose face will form its shape in my head?
Whose accents will fall from my lips?
How will I hear myself speak,
when I speak through the teeth of the dead?

At Rydal Mount
(1830)

Dark wet and a piping wind.

The cattle are deep blurs
beneath silver crescents of horn,
whose faint, moonlit wavering reveals

all that is to be revealed tonight
of motion and form.

The bull bellows endlessly,
seeing more than I, it seems.

His fury draws me in.

Key
(1832)

There is a type of melancholy, pressing on pleasure,
that comes from the sound of familiar tones
when confined—by health, not choice—alone,
one eavesdrops upon another's leisure.

My brother reads to his guests. Each measured
syllable reaches me like a small stone
dropped on still water, atoning
for the morning's—*what? neglect?*—with treasures!

Now and then a word, a laugh, gives the key
to which of his poems is being spoken.
Potted primrose glows newly gold on my sill. Tomorrow he
will rejoice with me to see it woken.

Portrait
(1833)

When first shown my face, finished and framed,
I thought it a cunning pre-figuring
of what I will be, if spared by God for great age.

From the smiles and nods of William I see
it is no projection after all,
but what I now am—*how I am seen.*

Most mortifying, the eyes—
small, as shown, sunken in flesh abundant
from giving in to the hunger

that now rarely leaves me.
I, who once filled my drinking senses
on the fells and pikes with things strangely moonlit,
with the deadening drum
of a force after rain or the crisp scent
of a brown bracken couch, for drowsing

through an afternoon. Now weakness
and perpetual chill has me stopped inside,
shawled before my constant fire,

unable to stride those old ways.
From bed to window is my compass now.
This portrait will hang downstairs,

not here—I need no reminder near
that *this* will survive me—this relict.
God—help me bear the affront, and submit.

The Robin

(1834)

Without ceremony or appointment he darts
through the window,

pausing straight before my face to breeze my skin
where no real wind blows.

As though we have some kind of pact, or friendship—
which cannot really be. He,

a slip of feathered instinct, seeking, feeding, singing—
not *for*—not *to*—just *by* me.

And me, a prisoner, sinking and reeling, feeding
greedily upon the outside gusts

that scatter from his wings as he pecks my crust,
dips at my offered teacup,

before he leaves in his accustomed way—out, out, and up.

Laudanum

My brother keeps count
of the bottles

I know it

lest the bottles end by having
the measure of me.

This tincture is my bitterest bane
yet masters pain with such quickness
its drops seem sunk directly into my frame.

Mary calls it
my '*treacherous support*'.
I hear her whisper it.
What would she know of it?

Or of anything?

I know only that, without,
I am first bone-weary
then bone-numb
then ungovernable—
with passions, rage,
a fury so beyond
my ownership

I observe myself
astonished, aghast,
as a stranger might,

unable by hand or word
or want
to intervene.

They say I must write a letter
(Spring 1838)

What shall it be? Forgive my brevity,
believe my desire as strong as ever
though my power totters and is bewildered.
News—news, I seek it for both our sakes.
Old Mrs Rawson has ended her
ninety-and-two years of striving and bettering

and poor Fanny Hughes is in a better place,
while I, who fight and fret and forget faces
am here before the fire!

News—news! More I cannot summon.
The laburnum's naked pods rap at my pane.
The pine trees reel from their bases.

Wean

(1840)

Weaning piglets scream   bereft
sensing already

                              perhaps
the blade

that will unmake them
                    in the manner
they were born to be unmade.

Some days

                    hearing their screaming,

I compound my breath till it issues
as with hidden force

        forced   forward in an unmeant

                              squeal.

Truthfully—this is   how   I   feel.

        Laudanum smothers the feeling.

My brother finds my squeal offensive (Mary finds as he does).

They take my crutch away

while I am dense in perplexity   figuring

        —oh!   save me—

                              things.

Where is William?

(late 1850)

Untallied weeks and months have slid,
becoming   *what now is*

since his beloved face brought sun
not sickness to my room

and—out of any human season—
in his light   I re-bloomed.

Some days he would take
my poor, sore feet
between his palms   for
          brief relief.

Other days, conjoined memories
conjured their own release.

Beloved!

Odd moments, now,
I hear his tones
welcoming guests
below.

Mary says this cannot be,
reminds me
he is gone to sleep   with their little ones—

whose names are seldom mentioned now
—at least by me.

I cannot bring to mind their faces—
but know well enough

how phantoms can beguile.

       I know he would not leave me
       without reason.

What does she mean by   *gone*
or words like   *sleep?*

Drowsy, I call for—seek—
       his steadying, loving touch.

Mary says he cannot, *will not* come,
but her eyes fly or flinch   each moment
at the ordinary creak of a door.

He is expected

I know it

       though

my heart   and   mouth,

like his

are dumb.

Last letter

(to Mary, in London, October 1853)

Dear sister—
a bearable night, though

weather rough.
Abed all day today

but well enough.
What do you think, Mary!

We have got us a new cow
while you are gone

and good milk she gives.
Rich and sweet, Mary,

and rich-sweet filling
to drink. And London?

And you, Mary?
Enough to write of,

for the moment, I think?

Notes

The epigraph by William Wordsworth is a fragment of a poem written around 1800 (*Unruly Times, Wordsworth and Coleridge in their time*, A.S. Byatt, Vintage 1997).

Pledge. The phrase 'all in each other' was used in a letter by Samuel Taylor Coleridge, to describe the relationship of Dorothy and William Wordsworth (*Collected Letters of Samuel Taylor Coleridge* V1 1785-1800, Ed. Earl Leslie Griggs, Oxford, Clarendon Press, 1956 p. 452).

Letter to Jane Pollard draws on a letter from Dorothy to Jane Pollard, a childhood friend, July 10 1793 (*The Early Letters of William and Dorothy Wordsworth* (1787-1805) Ed. E De Selincourt, Oxford, 1935 p.93).

Letter to Aunt Crackanthorpe from Windy Brow, Keswick draws on a letter from Dorothy written from Windy Brow, near Keswick, to her aunt, Mrs Crackanthorpe (*The Early Letters of William and Dorothy Wordsworth* (1787-1805) Ed. E De Selincourt, Oxford, 1935 pp. 113-114).

Coleridge appears at Racedown. Dorothy first met the poet Samuel Taylor Coleridge when he bounded over the fence at Racedown, in Dorsetshire, where William and Dorothy were temporarily living. However, Dorothy's description of Coleridge's physical appearance in this poem draws on a June 1797 letter she wrote to a friend (*The Early Letters of William and Dorothy Wordsworth* (1787-1805) Ed. E De Selincourt, Oxford, 1935 pp. 168-169).

Goslar, Germany, Winter. This poem draws on information contained in a letter from Dorothy in late 1789 (ibid p. 202) and a letter from Dorothy to her brother Christopher on 3 February 1799 *The Early Letters of William and Dorothy Wordsworth* (1787-1805) Ed. E De Selincourt, Oxford, 1935, pp. 211-215).

The robin poem draws on entries in the *Grasmere Journal* of 4 March and 17 and 18 April 1802.

Unseasonal draws on the *Grasmere Journal* entry for 31 May 1802 (Dorothy Wordsworth, *The Grasmere and Alfoxden Journals*, Ed. Pamela Woof, Oxford University Press, Oxford, 2008).

The berry draws on the *Grasmere Journal* entry of 28 April (Dorothy Wordsworth, *The Grasmere and Alfoxden Journals*, Ed. Pamela Woof, Oxford University Press, Oxford, 2008).

Trench draws on the *Grasmere Journal* entry for 29 April 1802 (Dorothy Wordsworth, *The Grasmere and Alfoxden Journals*, Ed. Pamela Woof, Oxford University Press, Oxford, 2008).

By firelight. This poem draws on Dorothy's journal entry of 22 March 1802 (Dorothy Wordsworth, *The Grasmere and Alfoxden Journals*, Ed. Pamela Woof, Oxford University Press, Oxford, 2008, p. 82)

The swallows' nest draws in part on diary entries of 16 June 1802, and 25 June 1802 (Dorothy Wordsworth, *The Grasmere and Alfoxden Journals*, Ed. Pamela Woof, Oxford University Press, Oxford, 2008, p. 110, 115).

The opening words of *Erasure* were written by Dorothy Wordsworth in the Grasmere Journal, in an extended entry for October 1802, dealing with the marriage of William to Mary. The words were obliterated soon after—presumably by Dorothy—only to be deciphered by scholars in the 1950s, using infrared technology.

Home to Grasmere. This poem draws on Dorothy's *Grasmere Journal* entry dealing with the return to Grasmere after the wedding of William and Mary (Dorothy Wordsworth, *The Grasmere and Alfoxden Journals*, Ed. Pamela Woof, Oxford University Press, Oxford, 2008, p. 132).

Last entry, Grasmere Diary. This poem conflates observations made in several late entries in the Grasmere Journal (Dorothy Wordsworth, *The Grasmere and Alfoxden Journals*, Ed. Pamela Woof, Oxford University Press, Oxford, 2008, pp. 136-37).

At the grave of Robert Burns. This poem draws upon an entry in Dorothy's 1803 journal 'Recollections of a Tour Made in Scotland' (*Journals of Dorothy Wordsworth* Vol 1, ed. William Knight, London, Macmillan and Co, 1904 (Kessinger Legacy Reprints).

Sinking of the Earl of Abergavenny. Dorothy's brother John was captain of the East India company ship, the Earl of Abergavenny, which sank on 5 February 1805. John drowned, along with many of his crew. This poem draws upon the content of letters written by Dorothy, William and Richard Wordsworth, to family and friends, in the wake of John's death (*The Early Letters of William and Dorothy Wordsworth* (1787-1805) Ed. E De Selincourt, Oxford, 1935, pp. 446-478).

Mean. This poem draws upon an anecdote of Thomas De Quincey, retold in his *Reminiscences of the English Lake Poets*, J.M. Dent and Sons, London, 1923, p. 101.

Coleridge in Difficulty. Coleridge frequently confided in Dorothy and William regarding his marriage difficulties and his poor health, and it is clear from the diaries and letters that the brother and sister were deeply affected by their friend's unhappiness (including his unrequited love for Mary Wordsworth's sister, Sara). The reference in this poem to Dorothy's 'nervous blubbing' over Coleridge is contained in a Grasmere Diary entry as early as November 1801, while Coleridge's written confidences regarding his failing marriage continued as late as 1806, when he wrote to inform them that the couple had formally separated (*Collected Letters of Samuel Taylor Coleridge* V2, Ed. Earl Leslie Griggs, Oxford, Clarendon Press, 1956 p. 1200).

Grasmere Churchyard. This poem draws upon letters from Dorothy to her friends Catherine Clarkson, Thomas De Quincey and Jane Marshall, between 5 June and 23 June 1812 (*The Early Letters of William and Dorothy Wordsworth* (1787-1805) Ed. E De Selincourt, Oxford, 1935, pp. 502-512) and also makes use of letters from William to Basil Montagu, Thomas De Quincey and Daniel Stewart between December 1 and December 22 1812 (*Early Letters* pp. 524-526) and from Dorothy to Mrs Cookson and Catherine Clarkson (*Early letters* pp. 528-536).

Final extraction. In 1820 Dorothy had her remaining teeth extracted and was fitted with dentures, possibly (given the cost) made with human teeth. This poem draws on letters to friends (*The Letters of William and Dorothy Wordsworth. The Middle Years Vol. 2* (August 1811-1820) Ed E. De Selincourt. Clarendon Press. Oxford. 1937, pp. 864-872).

The Robin. This poem draws on information in a letter from Mary to Jane Marshall in December 1834 and other references to a robin that visited Dorothy when she was largely confined to her room with poor health (Pamela Woof, 'Dorothy Wordsworth and Old Age'. *The Wordsworth Circle.* Vol 46 No 3 Summer 2015 p. 162).

Laudanum. Many references are made to Dorothy's dependence upon Laudanum, including in letters from William to Christopher Wordsworth and Crabb-Robinson in late 1835, when efforts were being made to wean her from the substance (Pamela Woof, 'Dorothy Wordsworth and Old Age'. *The Wordsworth Circle.* Vol 46 No 3 Summer 2015 p. 164)).

They say I must write a letter. This poem draws on a letter Dorothy wrote to her niece Dora in the spring of 1838 (*The Letters of William and Dorothy Wordsworth. The Later Years.* Volume 2 (1831-1840). Ed. E De Selincourt. The Clarendon Press. Oxford. 1939. P. 930).

Where is William? William died on 23 April 1850.

Last letter. According to Pamela Woof, Dorothy's last-known letter was written in October 1853, addressed to Mary, who was visiting London at the time. (Pamela Woof, 'Dorothy Wordsworth and Old Age'. *The Wordsworth Circle.* Vol 46 No 3 Summer 2015 p. 174).

Acknowledgments (and an explanation)

In 2017, I walked from St Bees, on the west coast of England, to Robin Hood's Bay, on the east coast—a popular multi-day trail known as the Coast to Coast Walk. The route traverses the Lake District, the Yorkshire Downs and the North York Moors, and I suppose I am not the first person to undertake the walk with a book of verse by the Lake District poets in my pack. The Lake District portion of the walk passes through Grasmere, where Dorothy and William Wordsworth settled at the end of 1799, and where Dorothy began the most famous of her journals.

I walked away from Grasmere with a biography of Dorothy adding to the weight of my pack. As the months passed, back home from my travels, I wanted to know more about Dorothy—to read her own journals and extensive correspondence, as well as the substantial literary scholarship dedicated to her, and to the significant role she played in William's life.

It may seem perverse, if not provocative, to presume to impose a poetic voice upon a historical figure whose own voice is well-known through her journals, and who publicly disclaimed any desire to be a poet (though Dorothy did in fact write a small number of poems that read mainly as cautionary or instructive tales for children). With Dorothy, there was the added complexity of her voice changing over time, as her mental health deteriorated.

Alas, I could not help myself. Nor could I resist the temptation to explore the sibling attachment between Dorothy and William that is at the heart of these poems, a love so crucial to the lives of both, from their teenage years until their deaths.

I acknowledge the wonderful National Library of Australia, where I spent hundreds of hours researching Dorothy, William, their times, and their circle of family and friends.

I would also like to thank for their generosity and encouragement those who have provided detailed feedback on individual poems and the final manuscript—Michael Wellham, Russ Erwin and Paul Hetherington—and all the members of the Molonglo Writers writing group, who will no doubt be glad to see the back of my obsession.

Deepest thanks also to Shane Strange, a publisher in a million.

About the author

Penelope Layland is a poet and editor who has worked over the years as a journalist, speechwriter, political staffer and communications professional.

www.ingramcontent.com/pod-product-compliance
Ingram Content Group Australia Pty Ltd
76 Discovery Rd, Dandenong South VIC 3175, AU
AUHW020721050325
407891AU00005B/31

9 780645 356311